Edmund Rogers, H. Piercy Watson

The Bridal Lay

A cantata with pianoforte accompaniment in commemoration of the marriage of H.R.H. the Duke of Edinburgh to the Grand Duchess Marie Alexandrova of Russia

Edmund Rogers, H. Piercy Watson

The Bridal Lay
A cantata with pianoforte accompaniment in commemoration of the marriage of H.R.H. the Duke of Edinburgh to the Grand Duchess Marie Alexandrova of Russia

ISBN/EAN: 9783744796002

Printed in Europe, USA, Canada, Australia, Japan

Cover: Foto ©ninafisch / pixelio.de

More available books at **www.hansebooks.com**

Dedicated by Special Permission
TO
H.R.H. THE DUKE OF EDINBURGH, K.G., &c.&c

"THE BRIDAL LAY."

A CANTATA
WITH
Pianoforte Accompaniment

IN COMMEMORATION OF THE MARRIAGE OF

H.R.H. THE DUKE OF EDINBURGH
TO
THE GRAND DUCHESS MARIE ALEXANDROVNA OF RUSSIA.

The Libretto by

H. PIERCY WATSON
(Jesus College, Cambridge)

The Music Composed
BY
EDMUND ROGERS,
Organist & Director of the Choir, St. Thomas' Church, Portman Square

ENT. STA. HALL   PRICE 5/- NETT

London:
WEEKES & CO.
16, HANOVER STREET, REGENT STREET, W.

CHARACTERS

The Bride	.	*Soprano.*	The Bridegroom . . . . . *Tenor.*
The Mother of the Bride.		*Contralto.*	The Father of the Bride *Bass.*

Chorus, Peasants, &c.

1. INTRODUCTION.

2. CHORUS.

Ye bells, ring out with joyful sound,
Let mirth and gladness reign around:
Come one, come all, and raise the lay
To celebrate the bridal day.
Come, maids and matrons, men and boys,
Shout loud, and wish them nuptial joys;
O, let all voices loudly ring,
While welcome to the bride we sing.
    Then ring, ye bells, both loud and long,
    Your cheering, clashing, mad ding-dong;
    Ding-dong, ding-dong, change not the lay,
    Ding-dong, for 'tis the wedding day.

Ye children, strew the flowers of spring;
Ye elders, goodly presents bring;
Let one and all to-day unite
To make the wedding morning bright.
See now the sun, with golden ray,
Its homage to the bride doth pay;
Then pray that those to-day made one
In joy and health their course may run.
    Then ring, ye bells, both loud and long,
    Your cheering, clashing, mad ding-dong;
    Ding-dong, ding-dong, change not the lay,
    Ding-dong, for 'tis the wedding day.

3. SOLO . . . . THE BRIDEGROOM . . . . . . *Tenor.*

Lov'd one, from this happy day
All our sorrows pass away;
Since in one short hour shall we
Each to other wedded be.
We shall know no care apart,
One in flesh, and one in heart.
Henceforth all that troubles thee,
Such will also trouble me;
And if aught give thee delight,
My life this shall render bright.
From to-day our ev'ry thought
To each other will be brought;

All the joys our hearts can know,
While we sojourn here below;
All the blessings from above,
We will share in tend'rest love;
That, as long as we shall live,
We may keep the vows we give:
I to love and succour thee;
Thou thy will to bend to me;
Whether sickness or good health,
Whether poverty or wealth,
Here for us have been prepared,
Cheerfully they shall be shared.

4. SERENADE . . . . *Men's Voices.*

The bridal sun is dawning,
O, bride, unlock thine eyes!
The golden streaks of morning
Call thee from dreams to rise.
Then lie no longer sleeping,
But look forth on the day;
And, through the curtains peeping,
Thou'lt hear all nature say:
Come forth, come forth, from dreams arise,
From sleep, fair maid, unlock thine eyes.

Then, nature's call obeying,
Sweet maiden, leave thy rest;
For she her welcome's paying,
Decked out in all her best.
Then may this happy dawning
Sure token be to thee,
That life will, like this morning,
From storms and clouds be free.
Come forth, come forth, from dreams arise,
From sleep, fair maid, unlock thine eyes.

5. CHORUS OF MAIDENS.

The morn, fair bride, breaks bright and clear,
    All joy and health be thine;
O, may the sun of happiness
    For ever on yon shine!
O, may there be no clouds to hide
    From you its shining rays;
And may no angry storms disturb
    The quiet of your days!

The sun of nature soon may set,
    And soon dark night appear;
Dark clouds across the sky may sweep,
    The raging storm draw near.
But may your sun of joy ne'er set,
    And ne'er give place to night;
May no dark clouds or raging storms
    Its brightness put to flight!

6. SOLO . . . . . THE BRIDE . . . . *Soprano.*

I hear sweet voices calling me,
    From dreams of night to rise;
And in those voices sweet I hear
    The tones of him I prize.
With words of tend'rest love and joy,
    He comes my heart to cheer;
To tell me—oh, what happiness!
    Our wedding morn is here.

Away, then, dreams and peaceful sleep!
    I will no longer stay,
By these enthralled, while others raise
    Aloud my bridal lay.
I will go forth to meet my love,
    And henceforth heart to heart,
We will in this world pass our lives,
    Until in death we part.

7. DUET . . . THE BRIDE AND BRIDEGROOM . . *Soprano and Tenor.*

The Bride.

The BRIDEGROOM.
My heart, dearest, is thine own,
Other sway hath it not known ;
Let, oh ! let, then, in return,
Thine for me with true love burn.
Mine with love doth burn for thee,
And from other loves is free ;
As thy love is ever mine,
So my love is ever thine.

TOGETHER.
Love's bright days now on us dawn,
With this bright and happy morn ;
One in heart, through life we'll go,
And no joy apart will know.
Whether sickness or good health,
Whether poverty or wealth,
Here for us have been prepared,
Lovingly they shall be shared.

8. PROCESSIONAL MARCH.

9. PRAYER . . . . . SOLO AND CHORUS . . . *Benediction of Priest.*

We pray Thee, Lord of power and might,
To guard these two both day and night ;
May he both cherish and defend
His spouse until this life shall end ;
May his commands, in kindness made,
By her be cheerfully obeyed ;
And, when their course below is o'er,
Bring them to Thine eternal shore.

The Lord both bless and keep you,
As long as time shall last ;
May His blest face shine on you,
Where'er your lots be cast ;
May He who now hath made you
Henceforth one flesh to be,
His favours pour upon you,
'Till death doth set you free.

10. MARCH AND CHORUS.

Welcome to-day this happy pair,
In accents loud and strong ;
Let one and all their voices raise,
In this our festal song.
In joy, in health, their lives be past,
Free from all grief or care ;
O, may the sun of happiness
Shine on them ev'rywhere !

Hail to the happy bride, all hail !
And bridegroom, hail to thee !
Your lives in sunshine now begin—
Bright may they ever be !
In joy, in health, &c.

All hail, all hail !
Ye happy pair, all hail !

11. DUET . . . . THE BRIDE AND BRIDEGROOM . . . *Soprano and Tenor.*

The Bride.

The BRIDEGROOM.
I will remain, my love, my bride,
For ever constant by thy side ;
From thee to keep all harm or care,
With thee life's ev'ry joy to share.
Shouldst thou be smit by danger's dart,
My love shall calm thy troubled heart ;
Should sorrow cause thy head to bow,
My hand shall smooth thy ruffled brow.

TOGETHER.
A life of love we now will live ;
And peace, that love alone can give,
Shall ever in our hearts abide,
While life we traverse side by side.
No angry word or jealous thought
Shall mar the joys this day hath brought ;
So shall we live in peace and love,
'Till called from earth to realms above.

12. QUARTETT. THE FATHER AND MOTHER OF THE BRIDE, THE BRIDE AND BRIDEGROOM.
Soprano, Contralto, Tenor and Bass.

The FATHER of the BRIDE.
Ne'er let the vows be broken
Which you to-day have made ;
Ne'er let the words just spoken
From heart or mem'ry fade.

The MOTHER of the BRIDE.
For ever may the treasures
Of heaven on you flow ;
May all life's joys and pleasures
Be yours while here below !

The BRIDEGROOM.
Never shall those vows be broken,
Which before the Lord were made ;
Never shall the words I've spoken
From my heart or mem'ry fade.

The BRIDE.
Love within my heart shall cherish
Fond remembrance of this day ;
Wealth and earthly joys may perish,
Love can never pass away.

The FATHER and MOTHER of the BRIDE (*together*).
Now for ever may the treasures
Freely flow from heaven above ;
Now may all life's joys and pleasures
Render bright your lives of love.

The BRIDE and BRIDEGROOM (*together*).
We in joy will share the treasures
That shall flow from heaven above ;
Whether life gives griefs or pleasures,
Nought shall take away our love.

13. THE FINALE . . . . . CHORUS.

Rejoice, rejoice, your wild huzzas shout loud !
May everywhere this happy pair
Life's brightest joys enshroud !
May their lives for ever be
Happy, joyous, gay, and free ;
May no clouds their sun dispel,
While upon this earth they dwell.

Come, more and more,
Your loudest cheers outpour ;
There's no man dare
Refuse his share,
Then cheer till day be o'er.
May their lives, &c.

May grief and care for ever banished be ;
So may their life be free from strife,
No dangers may they see.
May their lives, &c.

Joyous and gay
Has been their wedding day ;
Henceforth in joy,
Without alloy,
Their future pass away.
May their lives, &c.

THE BRIDAL LAY.

EDMUND ROGERS.

N.º 1. *Introduction.*

No. 2. Chorus of Peasants.—"Ye bells ring out".

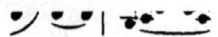

Nº 4. Serenade... Mens Voices. "The bridal sun is dawning."

N.º 3. *Chorus of Maidens.* "The morn, fair bride, breaks bright."

30.

Nº 6. Solo.—(THE BRIDE.) "I hear sweet voices."

Andante.

I hear sweet voi_ces call_ _ing me, From dreams of night to rise. And in... those voi_ _ces sweet, I hear, The tones of him I prize. And in those voi_ _ _ces sweet, I

Nº 7. Duet.—(BRIDE & BRIDEGROOM.) "My heart, dearest, is thine own."

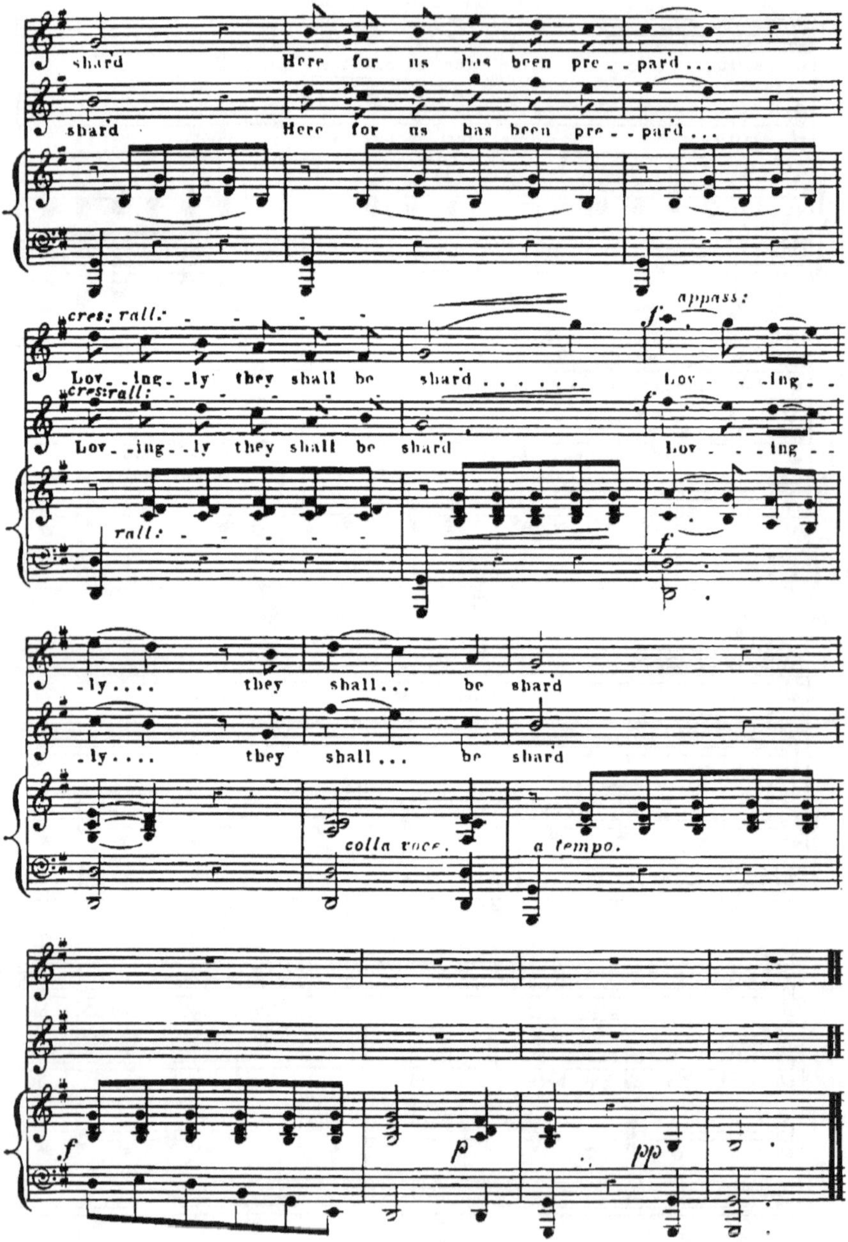
shard Here for us has been pre - - pard...
shard Here for us has been pre - - pard...
cres: rall:
Lov - - ing - - ly they shall be shard......
cres: rall:
Lov - - ing - - ly they shall be shard
rall:
appass:
f
Lov - - - ing - -
f
Lov - - - ing - -
f
- ly.... they shall... be shard
- ly.... they shall... be shard
colla voce.
a tempo.
f
p
pp

N.º 8.— Processional March.

IN THE CHURCH.— PRAYER.

Nº 9. Bass Solo & Chorus. "We pray Thee, Lord."

religioso.

Nº 10. *Wedding March & Chorus.* "Welcome to day this happy pair."

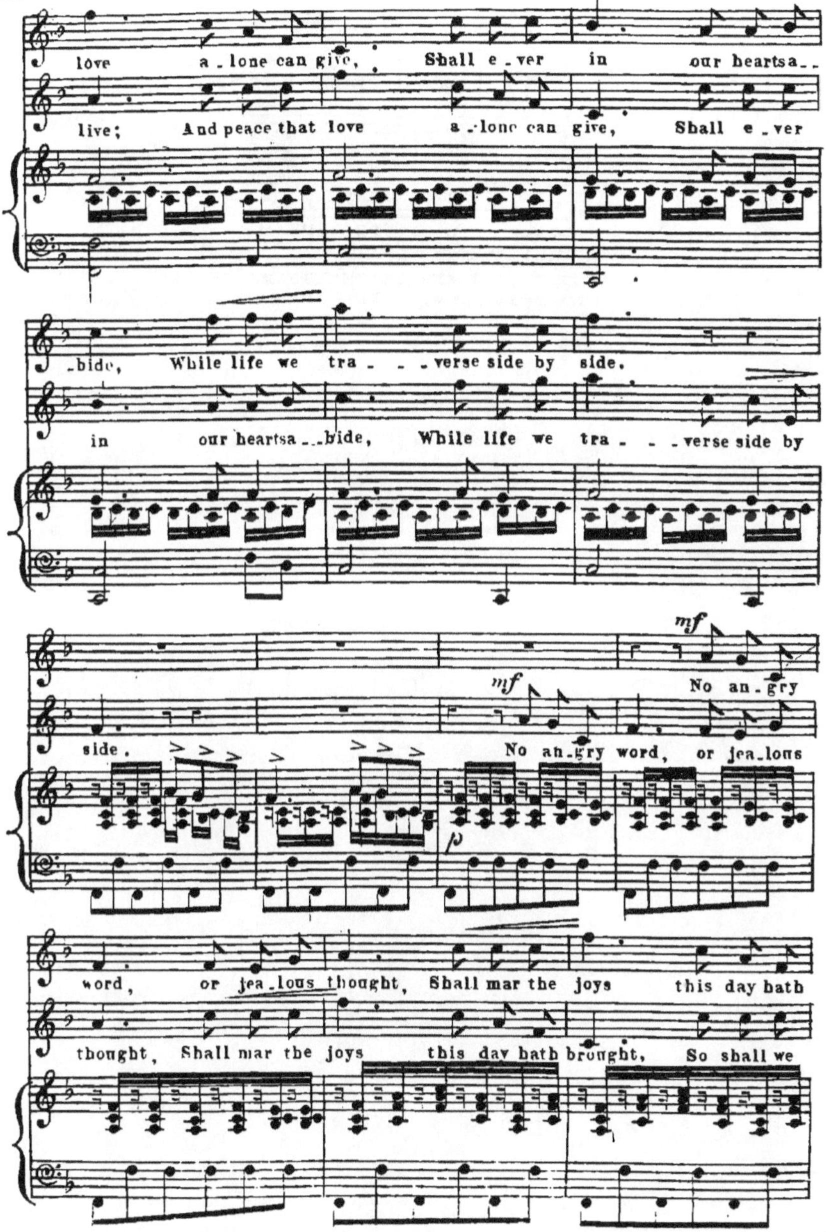
love a - lone can give, Shall e - ver in our hearts a - -
live; And peace that love a - lone can give, Shall e - ver
- bide, While life we tra - - - verse side by side.
in our hearts a - - bide, While life we tra - - - verse side by
mf
No an - gry
side.
mf
No an - gry word, or jea - lous
p
word, or jea - lous thought, Shall mar the joys this day hath
thought, Shall mar the joys this day hath brought, So shall we

78 N.º 13. FINALE. Chorus. "Rejoice, rejoice, your wild huzzas."

Allegro Vivace.

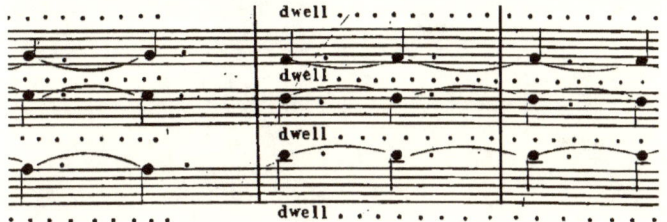

www.ingramcontent.com/pod-product-compliance
Lightning Source LLC
Chambersburg PA
CBHW031121160426
43192CB00008B/1065